Lessons of Winter

Nathalie Cortes

BookLeaf Publishing

Presentation by *BookLeaf Publishing*

Web: www.bookleafpub.com

E-mail: info@bookleafpub.com

ISBN: 9789357211581

First edition 2023

DEDICATION

For all those whose wings begin to flap when they are told they can't do something on their own.

ACKNOWLEDGEMENT

Gracias mama, papa, Kiko y Nono.
Gracias Joaquin por tantas lecciones en el frio y en el sol.
Gracias Gabo y Pablo

Thank YOU for taking the time to read this book. :)

PREFACE

The winter is not my home. I was born under the rain on a Wednesday in a country that has the sun's kiss all the way down one river and hugged by two oceans.
I wrote this because it's the first winter I embraced it as a muse rather than an enemy. A muse that calls for rest and often has more shadows than what we allow ourselves to bask in, I wrote wondering what would happen if I allowed myself to embrace lessons and even joyful things in those shadows?

Wind

Sincere
I stand as two women feel the warmth of the
tropic surround them
Controlled by motion sensors
where it rains every five minutes
and the coffee remains warm
and bottles of wine rest on the windows

We kiss both our cheeks and leave them red
drink coffees in the hot tub
making comics out of children's tales
We look upon the sky
the blank canvas greets us
we're alive and the hairs on our backs stand up
in the highest peak
the towers stare
change
begins as the wind picks up
the leaves move forward
and the naked trees remain in pose.

Fur

Bijou greets me from the corner of zotique
she wears a mens suit with boots from
L'iintervalle
and jumps from the fence to the ground to greet
me
She just ate two peas from the floor of the
apartment of the jazz musician

Beau Beau turns to me with his skin coloured
coat as I make a left on Beu bien
it hunches on its back claws staring at his
reflection in the cafe
down the street
Beau Beau has an owner who thinks their cat is
lost roaming
For a cat who grew up
Beau is actually just visiting

The Dance of the naked trees

A 4 pm we packed our weapons
we'd protect ourselves with paper and wait for
the sun to have its final meeting with the clouds
to wish us good luck
and write good morning letters hand delivered
on the snow
Using our hands to hug our papers to our chests
that the secrets learned once the sun goes down
sound different in the morning

The dance of the trees commenced as the trees
gathered around us
one by one swinging their branches towards the
sky
high and mighty
standing tall against the last of fall

Joyfully stretching with fury
a coreography of prey and man only
the ground glared at them both as the light bid
them goodbye

One by one their leaves came undone
in a pool of past paintings

gifting a home to those who protect what's left of ground
offering shelter for the remains of what has not been

They danced in the shadows
hugged tightly under each and dedicated a valse to the moon
who showed them their thickest corners were adorned by diamonds

J.O.Y

Just when you think you've tried it all to make
the cold wind not kiss you on the cheeks
you long for a warm embrace, another pulse that
begins to feel familiar
the devil will show up with a bubble butt and
offer you a shot

Texture

the sound of an apple
under your feet
and the ice melts in your mouth
and can be formed into the form of a fist

Mi primera vez viendo nieve

My first time seeing snow
I ran to hug it
i wanted to be a sculpture
and a shadow as big
as the trees under the sun
a sunny sunday afternoon
after a snowfall

A chimney

A conversation between the two
under flames
of missed laughs
from the visits of canvas skies

Community

We come close
because humans begin to feel
the weight of silence
from the sound of a crunching apple under their
feet
and the air has blades for fingers.

Holding hands makes it worth the time the cold
lives between our arms.

Honesty

an embrace of naked trees
bare your leaves
let me see how big or small change looks on you
allow me to document your creases
as the clocks mark below zero
one less hour of sleep
a morning to see an eclipse
to mark believing change isn't documented
in the stars
and dance your bones away with my
honesty

Truthfully

afraid of a bad moment where
we don't
admit
how our home should not abandoned
in the way we demand
for others to pretend to have roofs

Sonando

Suena el viento
en donde no se escucha
un susurro diferente
celebrando el cambio.

Alto

Cultivate the end of the heaven and above
the widest hug to impress in one single meeting
strong enough to last through years

Frio

el silencio de cargar baterias
en el descanso
entre las venas que regalan aire

The Blank Canvas in the Sky

One day arose
in the middle of November
where the air felt heavy
and outside remains blank
and fog embraces you
tricking a mind believing the campfire stories
were true
and the dust of change still held life for longer

Shelter

Sweetheart
in the purest sorrows
holding a still embrace of
memories
between our fingers
could be root of life possible

Finally

both elbows on the table
fill my cup the rim

No y si

Yes and no the depths of frustration

Suave

the end is rest
the end is rest and its
really worth the test

Hermano Mayor

Un corazon de leon
amante de la libertad

www.ingramcontent.com/pod-product-compliance
Lightning Source LLC
Chambersburg PA
CBHW051717130826
49812CB00034B/1231
* 9 7 8 9 3 5 7 2 1 1 5 8 1 *